National
Museums
Scotland

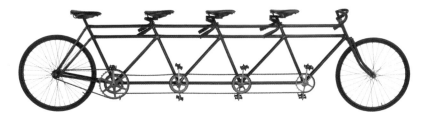

National Museum of Scotland
Souvenir Guide

National Museum of Scotland
Souvenir Guide

First published in 2016 by
NMS Enterprises Limited – Publishing
a division of NMS Enterprises Limited
National Museums Scotland
Chambers Street
Edinburgh EH1 1JF

www.nms.ac.uk

Publication design, text and images
© National Museums Scotland 2016 (unless otherwise
credited, see Acknowledgements, page 112)

ISBN: 978 1 910682 06 7

Cover design by Mark Blackadder.
Cover image: Window on the World installation in the
    Grand Gallery, © National Museums Scotland 2016.
    Page 1: quadruplet race pacing bicycle, possibly by Ariel,
    *c.*1898. Page 6: View of the Grand Gallery, image ©
    Andrew Lee.
Printed and bound in the United Kingdom by Bell & Bain
    Ltd, Glasgow.

National Museums Scotland has a Picture Library which
holds thousands of images of the collections. Images are
available to license for editorial use. Please contact the
Picture Library for more details on 0131 247 4026.

For a full listing of NMS Enterprises Limited – Publishing
titles and related merchandise, go to:

www.nms.ac.uk/books

Contents

Welcome

Welcome to the National Museum of Scotland. Founded 150 years ago, this is Scotland's largest and most visited museum, a must-see stop on any tourist's itinerary. It is also an essential part of every Edinburgh childhood, a source of inspiration and delight to everyone who visits.

Our diverse, world-class collections will take you on a journey through the history of Scotland, the wonders of nature, and diverse cultures from around the globe. Discover game-changing scientific breakthroughs and marvel at exquisite art, design and fashion from across the centuries. From the tiniest creatures to full-sized aircraft, from ancient times to the present day, there are thousands of stories to discover.

This guide is your introduction to the galleries, highlighting some of the special objects and stories you can find on your visit.

Opposite: View of the Grand Gallery.

Grand Gallery

Grand Gallery

Standing over 20 metres high and at 80 metres long, this large, elegant cage of glass, iron and light is a place where the cultures of Scotland and the world meet, and the arts and sciences intermingle.

When you enter this space you are in the heart of the Museum, the starting point for many journeys of discovery. With its glorious Victorian architecture, its soaring nave and sweeping aisles, the **Grand Gallery** is a dramatic cathedral to learning.

Above: Temple statue of Arensnuphis, sandstone, Meroe, Sudan, 100–50 BC. **Opposite:** Inchkeith Lighthouse lens, designed by David A. Stevenson, built by Chance Brothers, Birmingham, and James Dove & Co., Edinburgh, 1889.

Pages 8–9: Crowds in the Grand Gallery.

There is much to see as you begin your journey, most obviously the breathtaking **Window on the World** installation that runs the height of the space and contains over 800 items. The large, free-standing objects act as signposts, leading you towards the galleries. These objects include the Inchkeith Lighthouse lens, in use until 1985; the feast bowl from the Cook Islands, used at large, communal feasts; the imposing marble statue of James Watt, pioneer of the Industrial Revolution; and the skeleton of 'Moby', a sperm whale beached in the Firth of Forth in 1997.

The colossal sandstone statue of the Nubian god Arensnuphis (left) is a monumental reminder of a powerful ancient African kingdom that resisted Roman conquest. The Meroitic Kingdom in Sudan (c.800 BC–AD 350) evolved out of the first sub-Saharan urban civilisation, which conquered and ruled over Egypt in the 8th–7th centuries BC. Arensnuphis was a local god who combined Nubian and Egyptian symbols of power.

The statue originally stood guard at the entrance of the Temple of Isis in the ancient city of Meroe. It came to the Museum from the excavations of Meroe between 1909 and 1914, conducted by Professor John Garstang of the University of Liverpool.

Window on the World

Rising through four floors, **Window on the World** offers a glimpse of the rich and varied collections which form the heart of the Museum. Containing over 800 objects, sourced from the natural world, decorative arts and design, science and technology, world cultures, history and archaeology, this vast installation acts as a foretaste of the many treasures that lie in the galleries beyond.

The juxtaposition of objects from a range of historical periods, countries, cultures and disciplines is designed to create connections and pose questions. You can view the display from a distance or examine individual objects close up. All can be explored further using the digital labels.

Look out for the giant sperm whale jaw-bone, engraved with large images known as scrimshaw (1843), or the 14th-century Pembridge Helm, a headpiece that belonged to one of the knights of King Edward II.

You will also find this figure of a bodhisattva (right). In Buddhism this is an enlightened being who has chosen to stay in this world in order to help others achieve enlightenment. Often depicted in rich, princely garb, with high crown, flowing locks and elaborate jewellery, this bodhisattva is seated in the lotus posture and holds a wish-fulfilling jewel in his left hand; his right hand is raised in benefaction. One of a pair produced in north China, it was destined for a temple in Tibet.

Collected by James Fletcher, it adorned his house on the Black Isle, Scottish Highlands, for several decades before being presented to the Museum by his niece, Lilian Shaw-Mackenzie, in 1954.

Above: Figure of bodhisattva, gilt bronze, Northern China, possibly Ming dynasty, 15th–17th century AD. **Opposite:** A view of the Window on the World installation.

Discoveries

Discoveries

Sited next to the Millennium clock, **Discoveries** illustrates the legacy of ideas, inventions, innovations and leadership of Scots both at home and abroad.

Here you will find material that shows how creativity, innovation, and even accidental discoveries, by Scots have had a revolutionary impact on the world.

The influence of the Scots was felt through migration to the Americas, Australasia, Africa and Asia. For many, the Empire presented the opportunity to build a career, build a new and better life, or to make money. Some made ground-breaking discoveries and promoted ideas that changed lives and impacted on the development of our world in numerous fields, including medicine, mathematics, education, engineering, exploration and communications.

The objects in this gallery have come into the Museum's collection in many different ways and reveal fascinating stories of the people who used, owned, discovered or collected them.

Millennium Clock

At the entrance to this gallery you will find a 10-metre-high mechanical clock tower made out of wood, metal and glass. Commissioned in 1999, it was created by Eduard Bersudsky, Tim Stead, Annica Sandström and Jürgen Tübbecke in Glasgow. It comes to life on the hour, as its many fantastical figures and scenes whirl into action with music and light effects, illustrating the best and the worst of the 20th century.

David Livingstone

This gallery includes a display of objects that are associated with Scottish missionary explorer Dr David Livingstone. His collection is among the earliest African material to enter the Museum in the mid-19th century, and provides fascinating insights into the way of life of the people he met, as well as his own interests.

Livingstone had worked in the cotton mills in Lanarkshire as a young man and the display features the hand-weaving loom he collected among the Mang'anja people, from southern Malawi, in the 1850s.

Livingstone's reputation after death was marked by a number of memorial objects, including commemorative medals in bronze and silver. The small wooden cross on display is a fascinating example of relics and curios popular in Victorian Britain, the engraved label authenticating its link to the Mvula tree in Africa where Livingstone's heart is buried.

Pages 14–15: View of the Discoveries gallery.

Main picture: View of the gallery. **Left:** Commemorative cross in presentation box, made from wood of Mvula tree, Zambia, c.1900.

Natural World

Natural World

We are all stewards of the world's natural resources. To be able to fulfil our responsibilities we need to understand nature. The **Natural World** galleries provide a glimpse of the world's complexities and its wonders. They are intended to inspire us to learn more about the place we call home – Planet Earth.

Above: Lion family, *Panthera leo*. **Opposite:** View of the Natural World galleries.

Pages 18–19: *Tyrannosaurus rex*, cast of a skeleton found in the Hell Creek Formation, Montana.

At the eastern end of the Grand Gallery, a cast skeleton of a long-vanished *Tyrannosaurus rex* draws you into **Animal World**.

The stunning **Wildlife Panorama** is a highlight of any foray into the galleries, and there are many interactive opportunities to help you to explore the world around you.

Next to **Animal World**, two galleries tell the story of planet Earth. In **Earth in Space**, Earth's place in the universe is examined alongside the remarkable technologies developed by humans to explore the universe. The imposing Schmidt telescope at the centre of the gallery is just one of many inventions on display.

The **Restless Earth** gallery introduces the fascinating story of Earth's evolution as revealed by the huge diversity of rocks and minerals found on the Earth's surface today. The progression from a handful of minerals and rocks on early Earth 4.5 billion years ago, to the nearly 5000 minerals and hundreds of different rock types found today, has depended on an entire series of dramatic events – including the arrival of life.

Animal World

Animal World examines how animals go about their everyday lives in an amazing diversity of ways; how they move, eat, breed and defend themselves.

Most animals need to move around in order to locate food and water, to find a mate, to mount an attack or escape a predator. The body of every animal is adapted to its own way of life and its environment, whether it is the fast speed of a tiger in pursuit of a Sika deer (right), the wavy, lateral undulating movement of a snake, or a squid that uses jet propulsion to progress quickly through water.

Animals need nutrients to survive, and have developed specialised adaptations to feed on different diets. Some are predators, some scavenge, some graze or browse on plants, and others are parasitic. There are even animals that make their own tools to help them eat. The New Caledonian crow, for example, fashions twigs for extracting grubs out of crevices. Look out for the crow-crafted tool on display in the gallery.

All animals must reproduce to ensure the species survives. There are numerous breeding and reproductive strategies. A single elephant calf is cared for over many years, while a frog produces thousands of tadpoles that are left to fend for themselves.

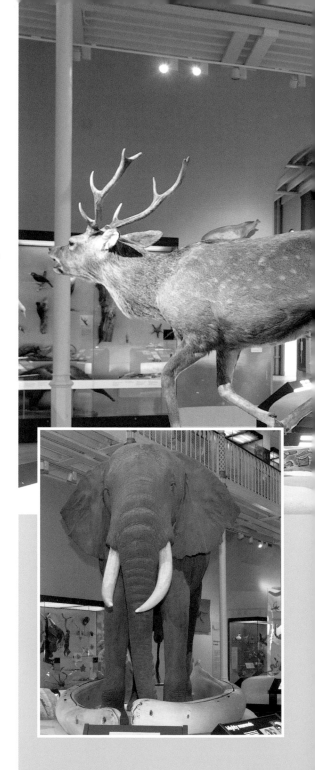

Main picture: Sika deer, *Cervus nippon* (left); tiger, *Panthera tigris* (right); with Burmese python, *Python molurus bivittus* (below). **Right:** African elephant, *Loxodonta africana*, surrounded by the lower jaw bones of a blue whale, *Balaenoptera musculus*.

Size matters

The extent of variation in the natural world is astounding. An adult male African elephant, *Loxodonta africana* (left), is the largest living land mammal. Weighing up to 6 tonnes, it has to eat its own weight in food every 20 days to sustain itself. In the display, an elephant stands within the jaw bones of the largest animal ever known – the blue whale, *Balaenoptera musculus*. Weighing up to 200 tonnes, the blue whale lives on tiny crustaceans known as krill, and may consume 4 tonnes a day.

The Etruscan shrew, *Suncus etruscus*, at the other end of the scale, weighs a mere 2 grams. It has to eat 1.5 to 2 times its bodyweight each day to maintain its metabolism.

Side by side in the gallery, an adult giraffe, *Giraffa camelopardalis*, at 6 metres tall beats the height of a giant ground sloth, *Megatherium americanum*, which became extinct about 10,000 years ago. The giraffe's neck stretches up to the gallery above.

The giant spider crab, *Macrocheira kaempferi*, from Japan can measure up to 4 metres across, while the giant clam, *Tridacna gigas*, from the Pacific can grow to a weight of 200 kilograms.

Animal Senses

Animals have developed an extraordinary variety of ways to detect their surroundings and communicate with each other. **Animal Senses** explores the development of a range of different senses.

Animals have evolved a range of senses to survive – sharp sight, keen smell, super-sensitive touch, and even senses that are beyond human abilities, such as infrared detection or ultrasound – to navigate or to detect prey or predators.

Colours and patterning are important and many animals use camouflage to hide, or bright colours to attract a mate – such as the striking display of the Indian peacock, *Pavo cristatus*, opposite – or to ward off a predator. Sound can be used for communication – to inform, charm, warn or to scare. Scents may persist and can be used to mark territory or attract a mate. The male giant silk moth, *Antheraea polyphemus*, has an incredible 55,000 pheromone receptors in each of its feather-shaped antennae.

Mimics

Leaf insects, *Phyllium giganteum* (above), are among the most remarkable examples of animal mimicry. These insects look so much like leaves – even moving as if blown in the wind – that predators will completely overlook them. *Phyllium* is not alone in adopting plant mimicry as camouflage. Leaf butterflies, *Kallima inachus*, are indistinguishable from dried leaves on the woodland floor, and the Asian horned frog, *Megophyrs nasuta*, with its flattened body and angular outline also disappears from view within a mass of dried leaves.

The bittern, *Botaurus stellaris*, has a pattern of stripes on its throat. With its head pointing upwards, the bittern's throat blends together with the reeds in which it nests. And in the sea, the leafy sea dragon, *Phycodurus eques*, has trailing leaf-like appendages which conceal it among the ribbons of seaweed in which it lives.

Above: Leaf insect, *Phyllium giganteum*. **Opposite:** The brightly coloured plumage of the Indian peacock, *Pavo cristatus*, is instrumental in courtship.

Pages 26–27: A procession of animals swimming and flying in the Wildlife Panorama.

Wildlife Panorama

Survival

Since its origin the world has been changing constantly, and response to change is a normal part of life. **Survival** investigates how animals have evolved over hundreds of millions of years, and how they continue to evolve and adapt to ever-changing climates and habitats.

In the process of natural selection, organisms that adapt to their environment survive, and those that do not eventually become extinct.

From time to time, mass extinctions have wiped out significant numbers of animal and plant species from the Earth in a very short period of time. The best known mass extinction event occurred 65 million years ago at the end of the Cretaceous Period with the demise of the dinosaurs, but the biggest extinction was just over 250 million years ago when it is estimated that over 80 per cent of all life disappeared.

Today the impact of human activities on the planet is accelerating and threatens the survival of many forms of life. A 'roll call' of extinction, showing the species that have gone extinct in the past 400 years, can be found in the gallery, alongside evidence of the threat to animal life from pollution, loss of habitat, hunting, persecution, invasive species and disease.

However, there are also some success stories of survival, where humans have been able to reverse the decline of some species by choosing to restrict certain activities and adopt different approaches to the management of the environment.

Fossil fishes and early reptiles

Scotland is well known for its diversity of Palaeozoic fossil fishes and early land-living amphibians. The armoured fish, *Pterichthyodes* (right), is one of many that lived in Scotland over 380 million years ago. Sometimes water bodies dried out, leaving behind layers of dead fish, such as the large block of fossil fishes (far right) from Dura Den, Fife. The 340 million-year-old *Casineria kiddi*, from Cheese Bay, East Lothian, is a special fossil. With *Westlothiana lizziae* (see pp 88–89), *Casineria* are regarded as the world's oldest reptiles.

Main picture: Extinct and endangered big cat skulls: American lion, *Panthera atrox* (left); Amur tiger, *Panthera tigris altaica* (middle); an ancestral tiger, *Panthera zdanyskyi* (right).
Below, left: Fossil early armoured jawless fish, *Pterichthyodes milleri*, from Devonian, Old Red Sandstone, northern Scotland.
Below, right: Fossil lobe-finned fish, Devonian, Old Red Sandstone, Dura Den, Fife, Scotland.

Earth in Space

For centuries humans have developed technology to explore the Universe and to try to find answers to the questions: What is out there? Where do we fit in? How did life on Earth begin?

Earth in Space explores how we use evidence from investigations to increase our understanding of these questions and more.

Since ancient times, humans have sought to understand our place in the Universe, to consider why there is life on Earth, and to discover if we really are alone. This continuing quest for knowledge has led to the development of complex instruments, such as telescopes and sextants, and ever-advancing technologies to enable a better understanding of the nature of time, space and the composition of our solar system and beyond.

In the gallery you can explore discoveries such as the key chemical components of matter and the way they combine to form minerals. Meteorites provide samples of the early Solar system; and there are also examples of the strange life forms that appeared during the earliest stages of life on Earth.

Above: Camera telescope, invented by Bernhard Schmidt (1879–1935), Sweden, 1930; made by Cox, Hargreaves and Thomson, England, 1951; on a base by Grubb Parsons, Newcastle, 1930. **Opposite:** View of the gallery with selection of historical telescopes, orreries and planetary globes.

Schmidt telescope

Invented in 1930 by Swedish-Estonian optician, Bernhard Schmidt (1879–1935), Schmidt telescopes are cameras without eyepieces. Thanks to Schmidt's revolutionary optical design, which gave a large field of view, they could be used to make atlases of the sky. This 1951 example was one of the first to be set up in Britain and the most used telescope in the Royal Observatory, Edinburgh, in the 1960s. It was retired in the late 1970s and the special glass photographic plates it used are no longer made. Schmidt telescopes are still used on Earth and in space.

Restless Earth

From the moment Earth first formed 4.56 billion years ago it has progressively changed and evolved. Each major development has left its imprint in the rock and minerals now found on the surface.

Geological processes have played an essential role in the development of life, and life has had an important influence on Earth. **Restless Earth** explores these changes.

A whole series of major geological processes and events has occurred since Earth first formed. Early Earth had a surface made of a limited variety of rocks and minerals, and a terribly barren and harsh environment, yet it did not take long before simple life forms established themselves. From this time on, life and geology have been linked. Earthquakes, volcanoes, plate tectonics and erosion have all had, and continue to have, an impact on life, directly or indirectly.

Life has in turn profoundly affected the atmosphere more than once. Each process and change is recorded by a distinct variety of rocks and minerals. Learning to read the stories in this rock and mineral record is a lesson covering millions and sometimes billions of years.

Rare Scottish minerals

Leadhills and Wanlockhead, villages in southwest Scotland, were once a major mining centre. The area has been mined for centuries for gold, silver and lead and has become world-famous for the variety of minerals found there, particularly minerals that contain lead.

The main lead ore, galena, was deposited in veins during volcanic activity about 350 million years ago. Since then, changing conditions near the Earth's surface have caused the galena to react with chemicals in air and water to form new, often colourful, and in some cases rare, minerals which have coated or even altered the galena and the host rock.

Over 45 minerals containing lead are known in the Leadhills and Wanlockhead region, including a number first identified from this area, such as lanarkite, leadhillite and susannite.

Above: Lanarkite, Leadhills, Lanarkshire, Scotland. **Below:** Leadhillite, also Leadhills, Lanarkshire. **Opposite:** View of the gallery showing amethyst geode, from Rio Grande do Sul, Brazil, 130 million years old.

33

World Cultures

World Cultures

The **World Cultures** galleries reflect the Museum's founding interest in internationalism and human creativity. The Asian, Pacific, African, American and Middle Eastern collections come from a number of sources, including Scots missionaries, traders, explorers and diplomats who lived and worked overseas. Today many of these collections are part of international collaborative research with artists, scholars and community members. We continue to commission, purchase and show recent work by living artists from around the world.

Above: Figures and camp dogs, Wally Pwerle, Northern Territory, Australia, 2006–7. **Opposite:** View of some of the World Cultures galleries.

Pages 34–35: Prayer wheel house, made at Kagyu Samye Ling Monastery, Rokpa Developments, Eskdalemuir, Scotland, 2009; prayer wheels, Nepal, 2009.

The **World Cultures** galleries are organised thematically across three floors. They emphasise creativity in all its forms – art, music and performance – as well as issues of cultural interaction and change.

Living Lands and **Patterns of Life** look at the role of landscape in shaping life and belief, and the manner in which belongings reflect culture and identity.

Facing the Sea shows the diversity and history of people living in the vast Pacific region.

Performance and Lives focuses on masquerade, performance and the social function of music; while **Inspired by Nature** and **Artistic Legacies** are more contemplative in tone, reflecting on nature as a source of artistic expression and how perceptions of 'art' and 'tradition' evolve over time.

From the 11.3-metre Nisga'a memorial pole carved in 1855 by Oyea Tait of the Nass River Valley, British Columbia, to the delicate jewellery made by Emiko Suo of Tokyo, Japan, the visitor can marvel at human diversity through tangible things, while taking in stories, music, artist commentary, and specially commissioned films.

Living Lands

Landscapes shape us as much as we shape them: they influence what we believe, what we make and what we own. Featuring indigenous communities from the North American arctic to the deserts of Australia, **Living Lands** examines the harnessing of traditional resources and the retention of ceremonial culture in the modern world.

Living Lands showcases important historic collections made between the mid-19th and mid-20th centuries from North America, Japan, Tibet and Australia. An early object is a bulb-topped whaling hat from the Nuu-chah-nulth people of Vancouver Island collected by Captain James Cook (1728–79) in 1778.

Important collections were also made by the Orcadian explorer Dr John Rae (1813–93), the filmmaker and botanist Isobel Wylie Hutchison (1889–1982), and Dr Neil Gordon Munro (1863–1942) who lived in Japan for over 40 years and worked with the Ainu people. Munro's collection remains an important material source for the Ainu today.

Contemporary art and personal stories are important aspects of **Living Lands**. Recent commissions include the Tibetan prayer wheel house made through the Kagyu Samye Ling Monastery and an Inuksuk created by Peter Irniq (b.1947). There are also works by Aboriginal Australian artists Danie Mellor (b.1971) and Samantha Hobson (b.1981). The Thunderbird transformation mask and outfit (main picture) created by Kwagu'l/Mowochaht carver Calvin Hunt (b.1956) of Fort Rupert, British Columbia, was danced by Hunt in 1999 prior to being sent to Scotland.

Tlicho (Dogrib) Nation

Between 1858–62, the Museum received several hundred objects from Scots working for the Hudson's Bay Company in Canada. This was in response to an invitation from the then Director, Dr George Wilson (1818–59).

Recognised as internationally significant, these collections offer a unique insight into the arts and lives of the Dene people of the Northwest Territories of Canada during a period of great change. Between 2002–9 they were the focus of a Scottish Canadian partnership project developed with the Tlicho (Dogrib) Nation. The project involved consultation with Tlicho elders and handling workshops, with Tlicho children as part of the outreach programme that accompanied the exhibition which went to Yellowknife and Ottawa.

One of the many positive outcomes was a contemporary collection which creates a new legacy for the future.

Main picture: Thunderbird Transformation mask and outfit, Calvin Hunt (b.1956), Kwagu'l/Mowochaht, British Columbia, Canada, c.1999. **Left:** Model hunting bag, netted babiche, tanned caribou side sections, skin thongs with quill wrapping, wool tassels, Tlicho, Northwest Territories, Canada, c.1862.

39

Patterns of Life

People around the world live very different lives, but share common needs, aspirations and experiences. Their possessions reflect their identity and mark important life events. They are evidence of the patterns of life that connect us all when we get ready to face the day or celebrate a coming of age.

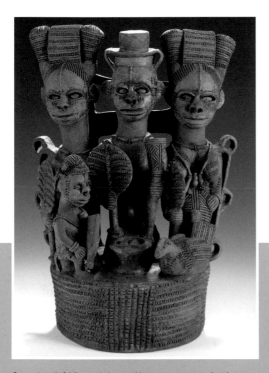

Opposite: (left) Painted shirt and leggings associated with Chief Wana'ata, Gros Ventre or Assiniboine people, early 19th century; (right) Black Leggings Ceremonial battle dress with leg moccasins, leather and German silver belt by Vanessa Paukeigope Jennings (Kiowa/Tohono O'odham) and Carl Jennings, Oklahoma, USA, 2007. **Above:** Clay altarpiece, West Africa, Nigeria, Aboh, Osisa village, Kwale Igbo people, late 19th to early 20th century.

Patterns of Life explores the dynamic interaction between people and their possessions. Across four geographical areas – Africa, the Americas, Asia and the Middle East – the gallery compares and contrasts rites, ceremonies and celebrations through special objects associated with them.

An object can bring generations together, as in the case of the baby carrier from Sarawak, Indonesia, which is traditionally made by the grandmother. Ceremonial objects, such as the wooden mask of the Mende women from Sierra Leone in West Africa, mark the transition of girls into adulthood; while the colour and decoration of a Turkmen woman's head covering (*chyrpy*) indicated her status in family and community.

The outfits on display were and are worn to express status, honour or religious belief. They include a battle dress (opposite, right) which was made and worn by the Kiowa artist Vanessa Paukeigope Jennings (b.1952) at the Black Leggings Ceremonial, Oklahoma, USA, in 2007; and the characteristic trousers of a Zoroastrian bride, a religious minority in Iran, which were made from differently coloured and embroidered stripes of fabric.

Harvest altarpiece

Many objects in the African collections were produced to be used in ceremonies associated with communicating with the spirit world. This elaborate fired clay sculpture (left), created over 100 years ago, is the work of a highly-skilled crafts-woman in the Ukwani Igbo region of western Nigeria and was used as an altar or shrine dedicated to the Yam spirit *ifijioku* during local festivals to celebrate the yam harvest. It appears to depict a chief with his wives, whose hairstyles, body scarification, circular fans and decorated drinking horn, indicate their high status.

Performance and Lives

Music, sound and performance are important to peoples' lives all over the world, from community festivals to sacred rituals. Costumes, masks and musical instruments that are part of these performances reflect long-held traditions, but also reveal how contemporary makers, musicians and performers reinterpret traditions for their own times.

Performance and Lives features masks from countries around the world, including Japan, Spain, Papua New Guinea, Ivory Coast and Sri Lanka. Worn for performances during religious festivals, coming of age ceremonies and community celebrations, each mask has its own unique characteristics.

One enormous ten-headed *papier-mâché* dance mask from Bengal, India, represents the demon king Ravana from the Hindu epic *The Ramayana*. Despite its size, the wearer would be expected to perform energetic leaps and twirls.

Highlights include early 20th-century costumes and masks worn by monks in Buddhist sacred performances known as Cham (main picture), representing demons and deities, in dances which communicate the legends and values of Tibetan culture. Also on display are larger-than-life character costumes worn during the Fancy Dress Parades held annually in the coastal town of Elmina in Ghana, collected for the Museum by anthropologist Keith Nicklin (1942–2002) in 2000.

Jean Jenkins, music collector

The gallery contains over 100 musical instruments, many of which were collected by Jean Jenkins (1922–90), a broadcaster and museum curator. You can learn more about Jenkins' travels around the world, listen to recordings, and even mix your own global music track using the 'World Music Composer' in the gallery.

Jean Jenkins' passion was capturing and sharing music traditions from across the world. She travelled from Bali to Mongolia, from Pakistan to Ghana, recording musicians.

A performer herself, Jenkins quickly put musicians at their ease and her recordings captured some extraordinary performances.

The field recordings, musical instruments, diaries, and over 13,000 images collected by Jean Jenkins, form one of the largest and most diverse ethnographic music collections made by a single person. This unique collection is now part of National Museums Scotland.

Main image: Costumes of Buddhist Cham Dance, as worn by Tibetan Buddhist monks, Tibet, 19th to early 20th century.
Right: Jean Jenkins, on fieldwork in Ethiopia, east Africa, 1960s.

Waka taua

When the *waka taua*, or Maori war canoe, was first added to the Museum's collection in 1854, it was missing a stern post. The most complete Maori water craft outside New Zealand, it was difficult to display because it was incomplete and seemed to comprise a combination of a river boat hull and war canoe side strakes.

Research has linked the canoe to Sir Thomas Makdougall Brisbane, Governor of Australia from 1821 to 1825.

In 2006 the Museum contacted Maori artist George Nuku to propose an innovative conserv-

Facing the Sea

The Pacific is a vast ocean, across which many thousands of islands are scattered. **Facing the Sea** explores the cultural diversity of this region. Living in this ocean of islands has shaped every aspect of Pacific Islanders' lives; here people belong as much to the sea as to the land.

Over many thousands of years, Pacific Islanders explored and settled islands from New Zealand in the south to Rapa Nui (Easter Island) in the east.

In the mid-16th century, Europeans began exploring the Pacific. Many of the Museum's collections were made by Scottish explorers, missionaries and colonial administrators. The collections include a Shelton Regulator like the one used by Captain James Cook (1728–79) on his first voyage, a Rapa Nui staff with two faces and obsidian eyes brought back on HMS *Topaze* (1868), and a Lou Islands feast bowl from the Admiralty Islands linked to the *Challenger* expedition (1872–76).

Cross-cultural encounters involved conflicts and misunderstandings, as well as mutual fascination. **Facing the Sea** features collections from Robert Louis Stevenson, for example, who made his home in Samoa until his death in 1894.

Pacific Islanders also desired to travel to Europe. Some brought prestigious objects with them to present as diplomatic gifts, including a rare Hawaiian cloak in the Museum's collections, made from thousands of bundles of tiny red and yellow feathers from the honeycreeper bird.

ation project which would restore the canoe, its decorative carving and shell inlay, with Nuku adding to it by carving a perspex stern post and seats. Maori people have always cared for their houses and canoes by repairing and replacing pieces when necessary. Nuku named the canoe *Te Tuhono*, meaning 'to join'.

Main picture: View of galley with suspended Maori war canoe, *waka taua*, Bay of Plenty, New Zealand, before 1827; with new stern post by artist George Nuku (left), 2008.

Inspired by Nature

Nature is an important source of inspiration, providing materials, forms and subjects for our creative expressions. In their works, artists and makers might capture the beauty of a natural shape, highlight prized material qualities, or comment on the impact of humans on our natural environment.

Inspired by Nature displays art from across the world. In four themes, the gallery explores how nature, its forms and materials, are used to translate ideas and beliefs and to express human fears and concerns.

Flowers, landscapes and animals are widely-used motifs in art. Terracotta clay figures, including horses, guarded imperial grave mounds in Japan. Legendary creatures, combining the body parts of more than one species, feature in mythology and inspire contemporary works of art such as Ray Flavell's (b.1944) glass sculpture *Kraken Storm*. Creative and destructive deities intervene in human life and shape the world around us. The Hindu pantheon in its complexity and diversity is presented through painting and sculpture. Nature is understood in its broadest sense and includes the social environment. Works by Jan Yager (b.1951) and Bhajju Shyam (b.1971) reflect on the relationship between nature and urban living. *Heart*, a sphere of willow by the Scottish artist Lizzie Farey (b.1962), is suspended from the ceiling. Farey added light to the willow to create a sense of calmness.

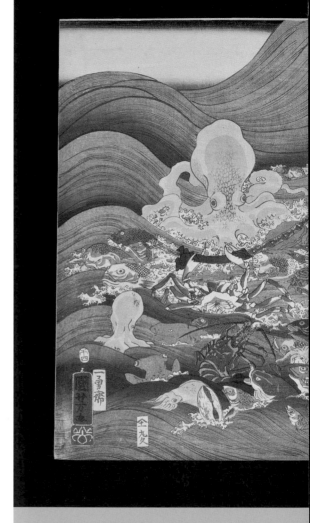

Japanese woodblock print

The 11th-century hero Tawara Tōda Hidesato descended to the Dragon King's palace and successfully slayed a menacing monster. Here he is depicted returning home (accompanied by creatures of the deep), together with his reward: a giant bronze temple bell, rolls of silk and a bale of rice.

Main picture: *Palace of the Dragon King (Ryūgūjō)*, colour woodblock print triptych, by Utagawa Kuniyoshi, Edo, Japan, 1858. **Right:** *Devil and Angel*, ceramic sculpture, by Maryam Salour (b.1954), Tehran, Iran, 2011.

Contemporary Iranian art

Contemporary Iranian artist Maryam Salour (b.1954) is fascinated by the transformation of rock, forming clay over time, which she can then manipulate and fire to produce her ceramic works.

Salour's sculpture *Devil and Angel* is a personal interpretation of the age-old concept of two opposing forces in life and nature – good and evil. The sculpture embodies her disbelief that the world is simply black and white. Both devil and angel grow out of a single lump of clay, unable to deny their common origin.

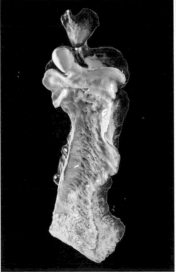

47

Trance

Preston Singletary transfers to glass the iconography, forms and symbolism central to the Northwest Coast carving tradition. *Trance* (main picture) is based on the traditional rattle used by shamans in south Alaskan Tlingit communities.

Main picture: View of gallery showing *Trance*, by Preston Singletary (b.1963), Tlingit, USA, 2006. **Inset, above:** Preston Singletary (b.1963). **Right:** Kondō Takahiro (b.1958) standing beside *Mist*, a monolith of porcelain with central glass element, Kyoto, Japan, 2007.

Kondō family ceramics

Chinese blue and white porcelain made for Japanese taste is called *sometsuke*. From the 17th century, Japanese potters working in guilds and with family kilns produced their own version of *sometsuke*.

The Kondō family in Kyoto has had three generations of potters. The first, Kondō Yuzō (1902–85), was designated a Living National Treasure in 1977. His grandson, Kondō Takahiro (b.1958) (right), has built upon the *sometsuke* tradition, developing a distinctively abstract, modern style.

Artistic Legacies

Art conveys the human spirit, culture and imagination. Nevertheless, what is perceived and collected as 'art' continues to change, and today the nature of art is hotly debated, with living artists providing authoritative interpretations of their own work. Their thoughts and views on the anonymous work of the past create a provocative commentary.

Artistic Legacies explores a range of artistic traditions from across the world, from antiquity through to the present. From Classical Greek and Italian pottery to the court arts of pre-colonial Benin, from Japanese metalwork to Victorian jewellery, from ancient Peruvian Nasca ceramics to tilework from the Middle East, the gallery presents artworks as tangible expressions of people and culture. Highlighted are the original ceremonial or political functions of objects, as well as factors which have triggered novel artistic developments, such as new trade networks, wider forms of patronage and political upheaval.

The gallery examines how different artistic traditions have been perceived and collected, and how contemporary artists draw on them today. Among the artists featured are British-Sikh miniaturists The Singh Twins, American Tlingit glass artist Preston Singletary (b.1963), Chinese multi-media artist Qiu Zhijie (b.1969), Japanese potter Kondō Takahiro (b.1958) and sculptor Gérard Quenum (b.1971) from the Republic of Benin. Through the displays, these artists provide insight into the influences, techniques and symbolism vested in their work.

Art, Design and Fashion

Art, Design and Fashion

Scotland's national collections of art and design illustrate the creations of European artists and craftsmen from the Middle Ages to today. The objects on display are of stunning beauty and show-case the most innovative techniques of their time.

The collection traces its origins to the Great Exhibition and the wish to show the historical creations of artists in order to inspire contemporary creators and industrialists. Items in the collection allow us to retrace the history of European art, design and fashion since the Middle Ages.

Opened in 2016, the **Art, Design and Fashion** galleries contain objects of great beauty and skill, showing how designers, producers and consumers have shaped daily life and domestic interiors.

The galleries also cover the process of making and creating, from the highly crafted pieces of medieval churches to mass production as it has developed since the 19th century. They embrace all the variety of art and design, from sculpture to glass, ceramics to furniture, silverware to jewellery, with a particular emphasis on textiles and, especially, on fashion. Great Scottish collectors, such as the 10th Duke of Hamilton, and creators, like Charles Rennie Mackintosh, Margaret Macdonald Mackintosh and Phoebe Anna Traquair, play a prominent role in the displays, alongside other important international artists such as Georges Braque and Pablo Picasso.

Left: *Triumph of Prudence* tapestry (above); console table (middle), Venice, Italy, top by Lucio de Lucci, *c.*1686–88, base attributed to Andrea Brustolon; table carpet (below) known as the Kinghorne carpet, England, possibly Norwich, *c.*1620. **Opposite:** View of the Design for Living gallery.

Pages 50–51: View of the Art of Living gallery.

53

Art of Living

A porcelain Meissen lion guards the entrance to this gallery, one of many amazing animal sculptures made for Augustus the Strong's Japanese Palace in Dresden. Here the visitor will find over 600 objects designed and used between 1500 and 1850. Most are Continental European or English, many with strong Scottish connections.

Art of Living explores the main artistic styles used between the start of the 16th century and the middle of the 19th century. Colourful displays focus on stylish living and contain objects associated with elegant eating or tea-drinking, in addition to porcelain figures and snuff-boxes.

The quality of the items reaches a climax in an area called 'Luxury and Magnificence' (right). Set against the chimney-piece wall from the Old State Drawing Room from Hamilton Palace, this concentrates on the internationally important collection of Alexander, 10th Duke of Hamilton. It also showcases the two outstanding silver-gilt services owned by the Emperor Napoleon and his sister, Princess Pauline Borghese, and the Hamilton-Rothschild tazza. Other star exhibits include the 17-piece Lennoxlove toilet service – one of only four from the reign of Louis XIV to survive – and the very large and rare Kinghorne table carpet of about 1620.

Two other sections examine the art of devotion, with an emphasis on silver used during the celebration of Mass, and making and manu-facturing sculpture, furniture, alongside ceramics by Josiah Wedgwood.

Hamilton-Rothschild tazza

The greatest treasure in Hamilton Palace was this elaborate tazza or footed bowl (left). While British ambassador in St Petersburg in 1807–8, the 10th Duke of Hamilton bought an exceptionally large Byzantine sardonyx bowl in the belief that it was the holy water stoup of the Emperor Charlemagne, founder of the Holy Roman Empire.

Back in London in 1812, the Duke purchased the enamelled gold foot from a gold monstrance that Emperor Philip II of Spain had presented to the royal monastery of the Escorial in the mid-16th century. He united the two and intended that this doubly imperial relic should become the baptismal font of the House of Hamilton.

In 1882 the 12th Duke sold the tazza and five other pieces to the collector Alfred de Rothschild.

Main picture: View of the gallery showing the chimney-piece wall from Hamilton Palace. **Left:** Hamilton-Rothschild tazza, a large Byzantine sardonyx bowl on an enamelled gold foot from the mid-16th century; bowl and foot combined early 19th century.

Design for Living

The ideas of design and designers, as we understand them today, were born in the mid-19th century. **Design for Living** looks at the origins of these ideas and explores how designers change the ways in which we create the spaces we inhabit.

The story begins with the Great Exhibition of 1851 and ends at the Festival of Britain a century later. Although the focus is not exclusively on British design, its influence in Europe and America during this period is at the heart of this gallery.

The development of mass production was important as it allowed people to own inexpensively produced decorative items for the first time. These objects are shown alongside luxurious and ornate High Victorian design.

In contrast to cheap mass production and High Victoriana is the Design Reform movement. Design Reformers such as Owen Jones and Christopher Dresser sought to improve design and design education in Britain. From that idea a series of artistic movements sprang up, such as Arts and Crafts Aestheticism, Revivalism, Art Nouveau and Modernism. All are represented by pieces of superb quality.

A particular focus on artists Charles Rennie Mackintosh, Margaret Macdonald Mackintosh and Phoebe Anne Traquair, brings many of the influences back to Scotland.

Above: White painted oak bookcases, designed by Charles Rennie Mackintosh for Dunglass Castle, Glasgow, 1900.
Opposite: View of gallery from grand piano, painted by Phoebe Anna Traquair, for Frank Tennant, Lympne Castle, Kent, England, 1909–11.

Mackintosh interiors

The celebrated interiors, which Charles Rennie Mackintosh (1868–1928) designed together with his wife Margaret Macdonald Mackintosh (1864–1943), with their pared down lines and use of white and simple decorative forms, were hugely influential on the design of the 20th century. The pair of white bookcases, designed for Margaret's brother Charles Macdonald at Dunglass Castle around 1900, was part of an ensemble of furnishings that expressed the beautiful simplicity of their work.

57

Making and Creating

The Museum has long collected contemporary work from up and coming as well as established designers and makers, and promoted new techniques and creative inspirations. This is showcased in **Making and Creating**, which concentrates on the work of individual artists and designers, and on the way design influences us.

The 'Key Makers' section of the gallery includes objects by Pablo Picasso, Jean Cocteau and Georges Braque, who all worked in a range of materials and media, as well as the British studio potter Bernard Leach and his followers. The best-known modern British-based potters besides Leach were Lucie Rie and Hans Coper, and their work is featured in the 'Studio' section which stresses the importance of the artist as designer and maker.

'Designing for Industry' showcases designers who are frequently used by large manufacturing companies to revitalise products and widen their appeal, and who have had an appreciable impact on how we furnish and decorate our homes. 'Pushing the Boundaries' is the culmination of this approach to 20th- and 21st-century design. Building on existing craft and applied arts traditions, the work on display in this section expands and adapts them to address the requirements of our time. Fashion trends, cultural movements, new materials and technologies are all challenging boundaries and demanding new creative innovations in craft and the applied arts.

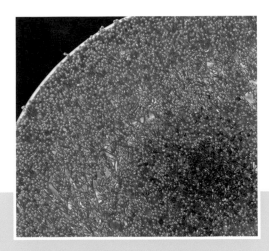

A hair's breadth

Internationally recognised as one of the most talented living goldsmiths, Giovanni Corvaja (b.1971) was originally inspired by looking at fibres and sponges through a microscope and uses a variety of techniques, including his own three-dimensional knitting, micro-welding and granulation, to form wisps of gold wire into sculptural jewellery. He is one of a small number of jewellers working exclusively in precious metal.

His knowledge and expertise has allowed him to transform gold wire, stretched five times thinner than a human hair, into the finest of fibres. The brooch (left) in the collection is 22-carat red gold and incorporates granulation niello, a technique never attempted before.

Since 2001 Corvaja has lived in Todi, central Italy, where he works as a freelance goldsmith and runs his private workshop/training centre.

Above: Brooch, 22-carat red gold and niello, Giovanni Corvaja, Padua, Italy, 1997. **Opposite:** View of the gallery with three glass sculptures by members of Memphis Milano, early 1980s.

Fashion and Style

Fashion and Style

Celebrating centuries of creativity and innovation in the design of fashion and textiles, **Fashion and Style** presents over 400 years of fashion history. It traces the changing spheres of influence and style, the impact of new technologies and cultural exchange, and considers the issues dominating the industry today.

We look at themes as diverse as the migration of pattern and design across differing cultures and textile techniques, and the changing ideals of body image from the 18th century to the present day. The transformation of the clothed body with exaggerated pannier hips, padded chests, outrageous leg-of-mutton sleeves, cartoonish crinolines and provocative bustles, is displayed alongside intimate developments in underwear.

The distinctions between the early tailor and dressmaker, the beginnings of couture and the growth of ready-to-wear are all explored. Many great names in 20th-century fashion are here, notably Elsa Schiaparelli with her 1930s Surrealist-inspired designs, Jacques Fath, Paco Rabanne, Vivienne Westwood and Alexander McQueen.

Garments from the preceding centuries include an opulent mid-18th century silk court mantua; and the oldest item, a finely embroidered linen doublet from the 17th century.

A changing display of cutting-edge contemporary fashion challenges our perception of what fashion is.

Jean Muir

In 2005 the Museum acquired the extensive archive of the British designer Jean Muir. In the gallery there is a spotlight on Muir, whose intuitive understanding of fabrics and instinct for colour amounted to so much more than the 'little black dress' for which she was famous.

Showcasing sketches, a toile (a test garment made of cheap materials, to test a pattern), paper patterns, jewellery, fabric and yarn samples, we explore Muir's approach to designing and making fashion, from the seed of an idea to the finished garment.

Featuring a butter-soft, navy nappa leather coat dress (left) and a classic black satin mini dress once worn by actress Joanna Lumley, the display reflects Muir's facility for combining luxurious fabrics, a meticulous attention to detail and superlative cutting to create the highly distinctive Jean Muir 'look'.

Below: View of the gallery, featuring *Rose Royce* hat by Stephen Jones (left). **Opposite:** Woman's coat dress, navy blue leather, designed by Jean Muir, United Kingdom, probably early 1970s.

Pages 60–61: View of the Fashion and Style gallery.

Hercules and Iole

According to Ancient authors, Hercules became a slave to Omphale, Queen of Lydia, as a punishment for murdering a friend. Overcome with love, he let Omphale take his club and lion's skin and sat spinning among her handmaidens.

The 14th-century Italian poet Boccaccio transferred this story to Iole, the daughter of King Eurytus, whom Hercules had carried off by force after killing her father. The myth became popular in the 17th century, and it is represented here by the Florentine court sculptor Ferdinando Tacca (1619–86), who specialised in making two-

Traditions in Sculpture

The human form is a constant subject in sculpture, with its challenge of bringing an individual to life in bronze, wood, stone or marble.

Traditions in Sculpture not only showcases many of the finest pieces owned by the Museum, but is also a short lesson in the history and development of figurative sculpture.

From the earliest times, sculptors have created works that inspire devotion, commemorate individuals and tell stories. The oldest exhibits include busts and statues from the Ancient world, figures of the Virgin and Christ, the Buddha and Hindu gods and goddesses, and a later marble bust of one of Louis XVI's sisters.

Many of the more recent sculptures in marble and bronze represent leading Scotsmen such as the radical politician Joseph Hume (1777–1855), geologist Hugh Miller (1802–56), television pioneer John Logie Baird (1888–1946), and the physicist and inventor Lord Kelvin (1824–1907).

In this gallery you will find a fascinating marble statue by 19th-century Scottish sculptor Alexander Munro, of the three-year-old Rorie Matheson as the infant Bacchus. Rorie was the son of successful merchant and trader Sir Alexander Matheson. There is also a statue, dated 1877, of five-year-old Arthur Thomson, walking naked along the seashore. This is by the French sculptor, Aimé-Jules Dalou.

figure bronzes of classical subjects. Tacca wanted people to place his small two-figure bronzes on pieces of furniture and to view them from the front, as though they were scenes taking place on the stage of a theatre.

Main picture: View of the gallery. **Left:** Hercules and Iole, bronze group by Ferdinando Tacca (1619–86), Florence, Italy, c.1650–60.

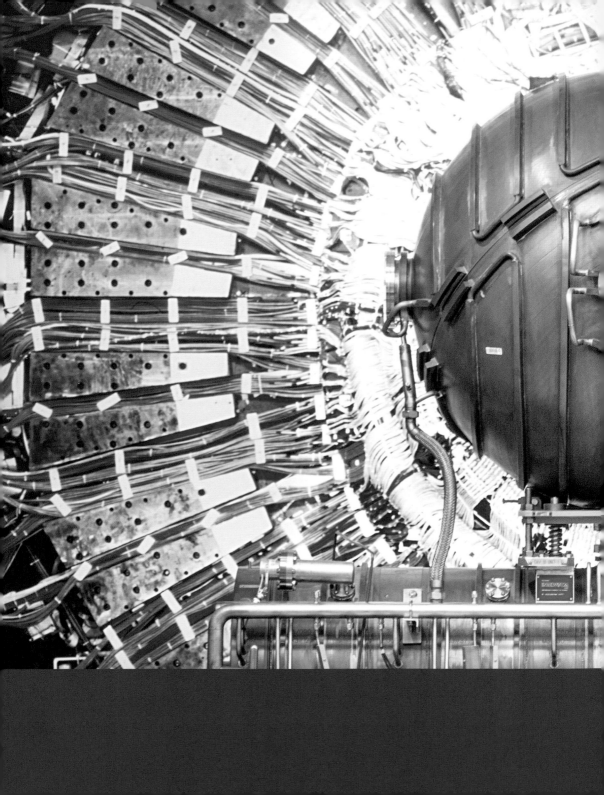

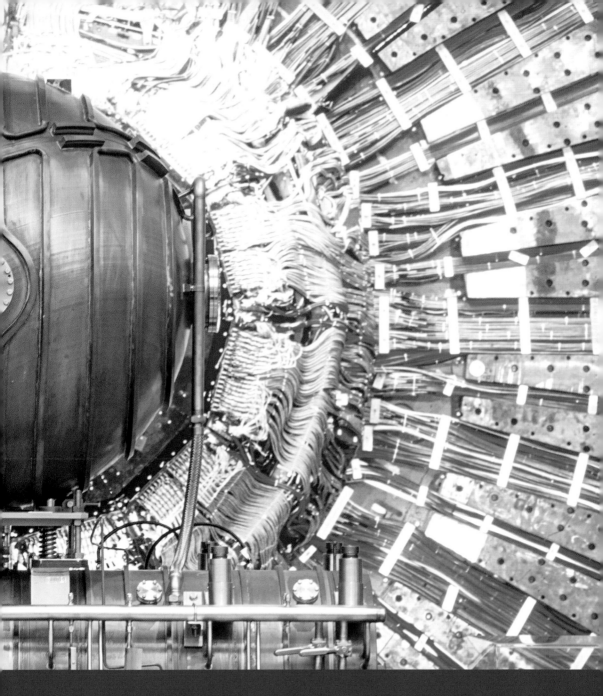

Science and Technology

Science and Technology

These galleries are full of intriguing connections – between science and technology, old and new, mundane and extraordinary. Stories range from the pure science that helps us understand the universe to the technologies developed in industry.

The massive 18th-century Boulton and Watt stationary steam engine and five suspended aircraft will catch your eye, but if you look carefully you will find molecule layer-thin graphene and a tiny mouse kidney. Such developments bring the story of science and technology from the Enlightenment to the present day.

From early on, technology has been at the heart of the Museum. We still collect cutting-edge tools and instruments, but these days our displays also include rockets and historic scientific treasures.

The Museum has always been famous for its working models and hands-on displays, and this tradition continues into the digital age with virtual interactives.

The combination of these experiences, and the thousand or so objects within these galleries, paints a picture of Scotland as a nation of innovation and enquiry.

Alongside Nobel prizes and world-firsts are stories of everyday people and everyday objects from bridge girders to mobile phones. From inspiration to manufacture to use, these galleries show how science impacts on all our lives.

Left: Visitor-operated hot air balloons rise up towards the *Gull* glider. **Opposite:** A plasma tube overlooks the Enquire gallery on the upper floor.

Pages 66–67: Accelerating cavity from CERN's Large Electron Positron collider (LEP), LEP operational 1989–2000.

Explore

All the stories in the Science and Technology galleries are reflected in this highly inter-active space. Underneath the Victorian glass ceiling you can get your hands on robotics, genetics, transport, aviation and the other themes that run through the exhibits.

Explore is a great place to start your journey through the past, present and future of Scotland's contribution to science and technology.

Some of the Museum's superstars can be found here, from *Wylam Dilly*, one of the two oldest surviving steam locomotives, to a Formula 1 car driven by David Coulthard, and the entire wing of a *Hawk* aeroplane as flown by the Red Arrows.

Right at the heart of the gallery is Dolly (main picture), the most famous sheep in the world. The first mammal cloned from an adult cell, at the Roslin Institute near Edinburgh, Dolly, born on 5 July 1996, represents a breakthrough in genetic engineering.

There are many more striking objects to look at, including the imposing Black Knight giant experimental rocket and the three-storey digital collections wall, on which hundreds of objects, images and details cascade towards you.

Hands-on activities are a feature of many of our galleries. Here you can learn about balloon-ing, programme a robot, control a levitating train, or even drive a racing car.

In full flight

Soaring over the exhibits in the centre of the **Explore** gallery are five full-sized aircraft. You can track the development of flight, starting with Percy Pilcher's pioneering bamboo-framed *Hawk*, the oldest surviving British aircraft. Diving below Pilcher's 1896 glider are a 1930s *Gull*, 1940s *Tiger Moth*, 1940s *Beagle* and a 1970s *Tomahawk*, showing the development from gliders through biplanes and all metal aircraft.

Alongside you will find a prototype of an unmanned aerial vehicle – an early version of modern-day drones. Together, these aircraft form a unique story of light aviation in one breath-taking vista.

Main picture: View of the gallery showing Dolly the cloned sheep (foreground), 1996–2003; stationary steam engine (left), designed by James Watt, produced by Watt and Matthew Boulton, which was used at a brewery in London until 1884. **Left:** View of the gallery featuring the Panorama of Flight.

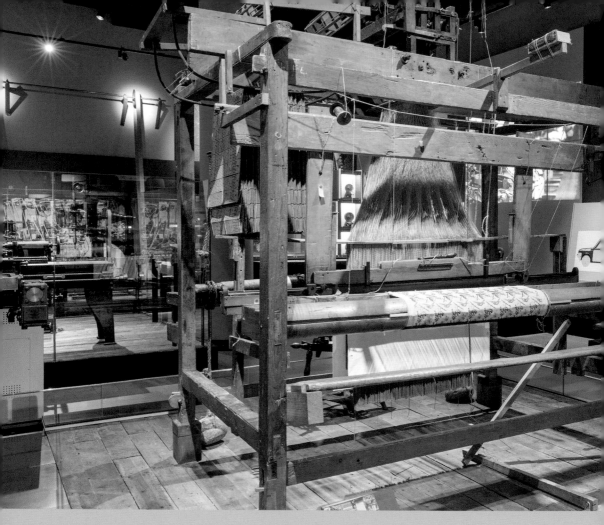

A model museum

During the late 19th and early 20th centuries, the Museum's workshop produced some of the most advanced, complex and finest working engineering models in the world. Early models include an 1880s Foster stereo printing press (above, right). The original, used to print the *Scotsman* newspaper, was enormous, requiring six operators at the same time – which is why the Museum has a model and not the original.

In other areas there are also intricate scale models of late Victorian steam engines, some of which are displayed alongside the real engines.

Main picture: View of gallery featuring a silk-weaving loom with Jacquard attachment, probably made by Joseph Hood of Newmilns, Ayrshire; and (right) model of Foster's patent stereo web printing and folding machine, scale one to third, made in Museum workshop, 1885. **Right:** Detail of the model of the Foster's stereo printing press.

Pages 74–75: View through the Making it and Explore galleries featuring an Argyll Flying Fifteen motor car, made by Argylls Limited, Alexandria, Dunbartonshire, Scotland, 1910.

Making It

Machines have transformed how we make things, where they are made and who, or what, makes them. From steam engines that powered the Industrial Revolution to clever robots and 3D printing, this gallery takes a look at innovations that have changed industry and manufacturing over 200 years.

From handmade items to mass-produced objects, **Making It** focuses on the technological innovations which engineers are able to create, and where and how objects can be made.

Exploring major developments that have transformed manufacturing processes, this gallery features a broad variety of industrial machines from 1800 to the present, alongside engines, working models and tools. They were built to make either one-off items or many thousands of parts. Visitors can also learn about the working conditions of a 19th-century factory against the clean rooms of microelectronics industries today.

Star objects include an early 19th-century Jacquard loom (main picture), which transformed the textile industry by enabling complex patterns to be woven, and an eye-catching 1910 Argyll car (pages 74–75). You can also see common-place machinery such as a large plastic extrusion machine and a contemporary 3D printer which is displayed alongside items it has produced.

Finally, **Making It** explores Scotland's impressive contribution to modern manufacturing.

Making it and Explore

On your bike

Prior to 1817 no two-wheeled vehicle had been built with the simple arrangement of one wheel in front of the other. The invention of the bicycle provided a seemingly simple challenge of designing the most effective way for a human to propel the machine. With three points of contact (hands, feet and rear) there are many solutions as to how a human can be fitted on to a bicycle or tricycle. It was not a foregone conclusion that the bicycle would take its present shape, as you will see from the variety of forms of vehicle on display, from velocipede to carbon-fibre racing bike.

Bridging the gap

Crossing the Forth, a major river, has been one of Scotland's largest engineering challenges. The different solutions are shown in the three bridge designs, from three centuries, in the gallery. Each reflects the technology and design skills applied to make best use of the materials of their time.

Main picture: The bicycle installation in the gallery, seen behind the *Tiger Moth* aircraft. **Right:** Scale model of the Queensferry Crossing, 1:1500, maker RG Model Services Ltd.

Technology by Design

Every aspect of our lives is affected by the technologies we use. Many of these have become such an integral part of our world that we barely notice them. **Technology by Design** encourages us to look at everyday objects from bridges to bicycles in a new light.

Technologies today are the culmination of big and small ideas, inventions and innovations – many of which are revealed in the stories of the scientists, inventors and engineers who have transformed our world over the last 200 years.

This gallery shows that these developments rarely follow direct paths. Sometimes the steps are clear to see, as in the progress from basic computers to today's tablets, and in the stunning improvements in prosthetic limbs that have led to the cutting-edge i-limb hand.

Other stories are more surprising. Research into radar, for example, has helped to improve both cooking (microwave ovens) and road safety (speed cameras); and the three bridges that span the Firth of Forth, built in three centuries, are very different to each other.

What is clear in every case is how much time and effort goes into researching the best form for these devices, whether it is an aeroplane engine designed by the Wright brothers or an artificial hip joint.

Communicate

Over the last 200 years, changes in the way we communicate have shaped our relationships with each other as well as with the wider world.

From semaphore to the smartphone, in **Communicate** you can explore the connections between people and the devices and networks they have developed to connect us further and faster.

From the wired world of Victorian telegraphy to the World Wide Web, communication networks have transformed our lives at work and at home.

In **Communicate** you can find out about the devices we have used to connect us to these information networks. The telegraph was the Internet of its day. It transformed the speed of global communication from weeks to minutes. Then, telephone networks made communication instant and personal. They built on earlier connections and remain the backbone of all Internet traffic. Today's wireless mobile networks trace back to the pioneering days of radio. The vast majority of all our Wi-Fi or mobile connections are only wireless until they connect to a base station, where they are routed through a physical web of cables.

From a telegraph pole to a satellite dish, our communications rely on the technologies which are displayed in this gallery.

Above: Magneto manual telephone exchange, used on Jura from the late 1940s to the mid-1970s. **Opposite:** View of the gallery showing examples of the modern mobile infrastructure, including a mobile tower hazard warning light and mobile antennas.

Effie's exchange

Typical of many rural telephone systems, from 1949–74 operator Effie MacDougall ran the telephone exchange for the Isle of Jura from her home. On call 24 hours a day, 7 days a week, she provided a lifeline for residents in remote parts of the island, and a connection to the mainland. Her Gaelic-speaking parrot, Patsy, kept her company and knew operator phrases such as 'number please', 'hold on' or 'you are through'.

Effie's manual exchange was replaced by an electro-mechanical system in 1974, one of the last in the United Kingdom to be automated.

Enquire

What is inside our bodies, inside crystals, or inside atoms? How can our eyes see something different from what we know is there? Science has provided ways of answering these questions, and more, and the discoveries made have affected all our lives through applications as diverse as antibiotics and colour printing.

Humans are curious, and science is a way of satisfying that curiosity, of answering questions. Scientists examine every aspect of our world, looking deep inside the human body and far out to intergalactic space.

This gallery is about scientists and their work, how they tackle questions and the results of their discoveries. Here you will find 18th-century chemical glassware (left) used by the chemist Joseph Black who discovered carbon dioxide; a tiny mouse kidney, only 3 millimetres across and grown in 2015 in a lab, which may revolutionise the testing of new medicines; and a 2-tonne portion of a particle accelerator from CERN (below) which has helped us understand what is inside atoms.

Enquire encourages participation in the excitement and imagination of scientific enquiry past and present.

CERN copper cavity

The copper accelerating cavity was a small part of the world's largest particle accelerator, the Large Electron Positron (LEP) Collider at CERN, the European Organization for Nuclear Research.

It is one of 128 cavities used to accelerate electrons and positrons (anti-matter electrons) to nearly the speed of light. Electrons went one way round the 27-kilometre underground tunnel, positrons went the other, then scientists studied the showers of particles created when they collided.

Above: Accelerating cavity from CERN's Large Electron Positron collider (LEP), LEP operational 1989–2000. **Left:** Glassware used by pioneering chemist, Joseph Black, University of Edinburgh, 1766–99. **Opposite:** Particle accelerator from a Cockcroft-Walton machine, 1950.

Energise

From fossil fuels and nuclear energy to wind and water, we need energy to power our everyday lives. **Energise** explores the different sources of energy we depend on every day and looks at how science and technology might transform the way energy is generated, distributed and used in the future.

Vibrant and energetic, **Energise** is a highly inter-active space. The sources, generation, distribution and use of energy over the last 200 years can be explored through a range of artefacts, touch screen and hands-on interactives. You can generate electricity in a giant energy wheel, make a splash with a hydroelectric turbine, and explore energy in waves in a 4-metre wave tank (right).

From wind turbines and solar panels to oil platforms and coal mines, you can discover different sources of energy and how their use has changed over time.

The future of energy supply and use are among the most pressing concerns in the world today. Historic dynamos and steam turbines are complemented by contemporary renewable energy technologies demonstrating how engineering can help us to find new ways to source, store, transport, use and conserve energy at both local and global levels.

The National Grid

On 30 April 1930 the very first section of the National Grid was opened with a connection from Portobello Power Station, a few miles from the centre of Edinburgh.

The development of the National Grid was one of the most profound technological changes of the 20th century, transforming everyday lives and industry. This isolator (left) was used at the substation which connected Portobello Power Station to the Grid. It is part of five pieces of high-voltage transmission equipment collected by the Museum shortly after the closure of the

substation in 1989. At almost 3 metres high, the isolator was used to disconnect the electrical circuit, making it safe for engineers to repair and maintain other pieces of equipment. Although parts of the substation were replaced over time, this section dates from the opening of the National Grid in 1930.

Main picture: Visitors can explore energy in waves in a 4-metre wave tank. **Left:** Cod-head isolator, one of five parts of high voltage electricity transmission equipment, recovered from Portobello substation, dated 1930.

Scotland Galleries

Scotland Galleries

These galleries tell Scotland's story, from its remote beginnings as a land mass billions of years ago, right up to the present day. From tiny flint blades to enormous locomotive engines, from humble possessions to the grandest treasures, the displays show how people have lived, how Scotland has developed and changed as a nation, and how Scottish innovation has helped to shape the modern world.

Above: Christian cross-slab, found at Hilton of Cadboll, Ross and Cromarty, 8th century AD. **Opposite:** View of the Industry and Empire gallery showing a single-cylinder horizontal stationary steam engine, built by Douglas and Grant Ltd, Kirkcaldy, 1923.

Starting on the lowest floor, **Beginnings** presents three billion years of Scotland's geology and natural history, including fossils such as *Westlothiana lizziae*, found in 1984 and possibly the earliest known reptile. **Early People** introduces Scotland's early inhabitants, taking the story from the end of the Ice Age to AD 1100 through objects such as the magnificent Christian cross-slab from the Hilton of Cadboll (left).

Kingdom of the Scots shows how Scotland became a nation, tracing its development to 1707. Here you will find a wild-eyed berserker chess piece from the Isle of Lewis and jewellery associated with Mary, Queen of Scots.

Scotland Transformed covers changes in people's lives during the 18th and early 19th centuries and highlights Bonnie Prince Charlie's doomed attempt to retake the British throne for his father, James VIII and III.

Industry and Empire deals with the massive impact of the Industrial Revolution and traces Scotland's role in the British Empire.

Finally, on the top floor, there is **Scotland: A Changing Nation**, which brings the story up to date by considering how Scotland has fared in a changing economic and political climate. This gallery holds a mirror to contemporary society.

Beginnings

The story of Scotland begins billions of years ago, long before it took its present form, and even before Scotland was in its present geographical position.

Throughout Earth's history the continents have continually shifted positions. Many millions of years ago the landmass that today makes up a large part of Scotland was located in the Southern Hemisphere.

The oldest Scottish rocks are approximately 3 billion years old, and Scotland's fascinating geological diversity has inspired generations of pioneering scientists, none more so than James Hutton (1726–97), known around the world as the 'Father of Modern Geology'.

Fossilised remains of animals and plants, including those discovered by another great Scottish geologist Hugh Miller (1802–56), have also helped us understand the geological history of Scotland.

Main picture: History of the Forest Diorama, Tundra in Scotland, 12,000 years ago; **Right:** Stem-amniote tetrapod (amphibian), *Westlothiana lizziae*, from the early Carboniferous period of East Kirkton Quarry, West Lothian, Scotland; and model of *Westlothiana lizziae* (far right).

'Lizzie'

Westlothiana lizziae (right), a fossilised vertebrate discovered in East Kirkton Quarry in West Lothian, Scotland, in 1984, is the world's earliest known amniote – it had a waterproof skin, and laid eggs that could hatch on land.

Living 345 million years ago, *Westlothiana lizziae* is crucial evidence for the early radiation of back-boned animals on land. Recent fossil discoveries in Scotland have clarified this critical evolutionary moment.

Towie carved ball

The 5000-year-old carved stone ball from Towie (right), Aberdeenshire, with intricate designs on three of its four knobs, is the finest example of a type of object peculiar to Scotland.

Around the size of a tennis ball, and with between three and more than 200 knobs, these objects have long puzzled and fascinated people. Over 400 are known, mostly from north-east Scotland. Made by skilled stone-workers, they could have been weapons, dealing a deadly blow when thrown at an enemy's head. But, they were first and foremost symbols of power, which were owned by a sophisticated and well-travelled élite.

Links with eastern Ireland are revealed by the Towie stone ball's spiral design, echoing that on the massive monument at Newgrange, and by the presence of miniature carved stone ball beads at Knowth, both in the faraway Boyne Valley.

Main picture: Some pieces from a hoard of Roman silver found at Traprain Law, East Lothian, AD 400–50. **Right:** Carved stone ball, Towie, Aberdeenshire, 2500 BC.

Early People

Early People introduces Scotland's earliest inhabitants, from the end of the Ice Age to AD 1100, exploring how they lived, moved around, formed networks and communities, and how they understood the world.

Combining modern art with ancient objects, the gallery uses the artefacts that Scotland's early inhabitants left behind to piece together a fascinating picture of their lives and beliefs over more than 10,000 years.

The displays are grouped into four themes, with an introductory area dominated by the massive Christian cross-slab from Hilton of Cadboll and a set of sculptures by the eminent Scottish artist Sir Eduardo Paolozzi (1924–2005). Look closely at these and you will find ancient treasures on and around the angular bodies of the bronze figures.

Further into the gallery, 'A Generous Land' shows how people have used Scotland's rich resources over the millennia, while 'Wider Horizons' explores ways of travelling around, and traces the movement of objects, ideas and people.

'Them and Us' delves into the ways people co-existed, from fighting with each other to lavishing gifts on loved ones and allies.

And finally, 'In Touch with the Gods' focuses on beliefs: how death was handled, and how people made sense of the world around them.

Kingdom of the Scots

The consolidation of Scotland's status as a nation from 1100–1707 is the focus of these galleries, telling the story of the kingdom's developing sense of identity and independence, together with its rising presence in Europe.

Within **Kingdom of the Scots** there are several galleries dedicated to this 600-year period of Scottish history, exploring the identity and characterisation of the country and its people.

By the 12th century the Scots were being identified as a cohesive body made up of a population of mixed origins including settlers from France, England and the Low Countries.

The beginnings of the Scottish nation were also profoundly affected by the spread of Christianity which helped draw the country together. Warfare was a dominant aspect of life, and Scotland's borders were maintained through an army raised by those that held land and money.

This process of forging Scotland into the nation that we now recognise took several centuries and can be attributed to the activities of vigorous and successful kings. The Stewarts in particular were a remarkable and tenacious dynasty who ruled Scotland for more than 300 years. In 1603 this dynasty succeeded to the English crown, establishing a regal union between both kingdoms.

Playing the game

The Lewis chess pieces are among Scotland's best-known objects. The eleven pieces in the national collection consist of elaborately worked walrus ivory and whales' teeth in the form of seated kings and queens, bishops, knights and warders. They were probably made in Trondheim, Norway, around 1150–1200, and were found in the parish of Uig on the Isle of Lewis, which was at that time part of the Norse kingdom.

The chess pieces have been the subject of much speculation since their discovery in 1831. They may have been buried on the island by a travelling merchant who was shipwrecked. However, Lewis was home to significant and powerful people who frequently travelled. They may have buried their possessions for safe-keeping while on a sojourn, fully intending to return at a later date.

Today they are one of the most iconic indications of Norse influence and connections with the country we now call Scotland.

The **Kingdom of the Scots** covers a large sweep of history dedicated to the early development of the Scottish nation and its people. Europe played a major role in the kingdom's advancement through the exchange of cultural and intellectual ideas, together with the emerging world of commerce.

The formation of Scotland and its identity was encouraged through its relations with Europe and its shared religious, diplomatic, economic and cultural ties. Many Scots were educated at the great European universities and returned home with a wide knowledge of thought and culture from Europe and beyond. This sharing and development of cultural ideas in the later Middle Ages became known as the Renaissance.

In addition to cultural development, Scotland's towns continued to emerge and thrive due to contact with England and Europe. From the 12th century, burghs were created to promote and control trade and manufacture, and in turn were regulated by guilds and craft incorporations. Burgh merchants exported wool, leather and fish, and imported items such as wine, beer, exotic spices and fine cloth.

As Scotland progressed from the medieval period to the early modern, it rose to the challenges of political tension, religious intolerance, armed conflict and economic failure. The latter was partly caused in the 1690s by the ill-fated Darien Scheme which almost bankrupted the country. The difficult economic climate of the late 18th century was one of the driving factors behind the union with England in 1707.

The Darien Scheme

This chest was the property of the Darien Company and has a complicated lock of 15 spring bolts. It was probably used to hold money and important documents.

The chest is one of the few surviving objects associated with the Darien Company, or more fully the Company of Scotland Trading to Africa and the Indies. Founded by an Act of the Parliament of Scotland in 1695, this was an attempt by Scotland to set up an overseas trading company in the style of the East India Company, based on the Isthmus of Panama, Central America.

The colony's failure was due to the Company's inadequate preparation and organisation, but also disease, Spanish hostility and the need for William III, king of England, Ireland and Scotland, to appease Spain in his war with France.

Above: Strong box, possibly German, 17th century, used to hold money and documents of the Company of Scotland, which funded the Darien Scheme. **Opposite:** View of the gallery, showing a clarsach harp known as the Queen Mary harp, *c.*1450 (left), and an oak carving of Saint Andrew, Low Countries, *c.*1500 (right).

Scotland Transformed

This suite of galleries is dedicated to life in Scotland during the 18th and early 19th centuries. It examines the fundamental changes and effects these had. Change was not uniform and for many, especially in some rural areas, life remained much the same.

In 1707 Scotland and England were united under the newly-created parliament of Great Britain. The terms of the Treaty of Union were to have a lasting effect on all aspects of Scottish society.

This was the age of the Jacobite wars, when the exiled House of Stuart and its supporters made many attempts to regain the British throne. The Jacobite challenge threatened the ruling Protestant branch of the Stuart dynasty and, after 1714, the new Hanoverian monarchy. It was not until their defeat at the Battle of Culloden in 1746 that the Cause disintegrated.

The 18th century was also a period of new ideas and intellectual enquiry. Known as the Enlightenment, a number of Scots made key contributions to this movement. It encompassed art, architecture, education, philosophy, science and technology, and the new social sciences.

These advancements influenced many aspects of life, including the improvement of agriculture, communication and the building of new towns throughout the country.

Bonnie Prince Charlie's picnic set

This canteen consists of a complete set of silver-gilt cutlery, including knives, forks, spoons, nutmeg grater, corkscrew, a cruet and two wine beakers. The case is beautifully decorated with chased bands of linked thistles, engraved in the centre with the three-feather badge of the Prince of Wales, while the domed lid displays the figure of Saint Andrew.

This exquisite picnic set was possibly a twenty-first birthday present for Prince Charles Edward Stuart, who was a keen hunter. He

was the last of the Stuarts to attempt to retake the throne, but his hopes were crushed after the Battle of Culloden in 1746.

His canteen ended up in a baggage wagon at the battle site where it was eventually seized by government forces under the command of the duke of Cumberland.

Main picture: View of gallery showing cruck house, early 18th century. **Right:** Silver travelling canteen belonging to Prince Charles Edward Stuart, by Ebenezer Oliphant, Edinburgh, 1740–41.

The 18th- and early 19th-century galleries of **Scotland Transformed** trace the significant shift from a predominantly rural economy and society into one that became overwhelmingly urban and industrial. It also considers the role of Scotland's churches during this period.

During the 1700s the majority of people in Scotland were engaged in agriculture. Industrial progress was sporadic, and far from uniform, until the end of the 18th century.

However, developments in technology had an enormous impact and changed the country's main source of power from water to steam. This transformed several areas of industry including coal and textile production, with the latter seeing a transition from hand to water to steam power.

The role of the Church of Scotland in society, especially in terms of its doctrine and social provision, was all-encompassing. As the country's established church, it clashed with those outside of it, such as Episcopalians, Catholics and Protestant dissenters. Its assertion of independence from state control and the influence of wealthy landowners brought tension with government, and growing internal division. The issues culminated in a dramatic split, the Disruption of 1843.

Spiritual life reflected an age where illness and the presence of death were always close. The conventions of death and mourning became more elaborate, while folk belief in supernatural forces endured.

Arthur's Seat coffins

A chance find in 1836 uncovered these mysterious objects, which have fascinated generations of visitors, but whose essential mystery has never been resolved. Tucked into a crevice on Arthur's Seat, Edinburgh's landmark hill, some schoolboys found 17 miniature coffins, eight of which survive today. Carefully made and decorated from pine and tin, and each containing a wooden figure of a corpse dressed in linen and cotton clothing, scientific testing indicates they were probably made and concealed only a few years before they were found. Theories of what they were meant to represent run from witchcraft and folk traditions to a private expression of grief. They have featured in the work of the celebrated Edinburgh-based crime writer Ian Rankin. Perhaps the most plausible explanation is a connection to the sensational 1829 trial of Edinburgh murderers William Burke and William Hare, who sold the bodies of 17 of their victims for surgical dissection.

Above: Miniature coffins with lids and carved figures, found on Arthur's Seat, Edinburgh, June 1836. **Opposite:** View of the gallery with Newcomen atmospheric engine from Caprington Colliery, near Kilmarnock, Ayrshire, in use 1811–1901.

Lighthouse Stevenson

One of Scotland's most famous engineers, Robert Stevenson designed the Bell Rock lighthouse, a model of which is in the gallery. The building of this lighthouse in tidal waters off the east coast of Scotland was truly remarkable.

The rocks had been responsible for many shipwrecks and in 1799 Stevenson proposed a lighthouse. Concerns about cost and the young age of the engineer caused considerable delay, but approval was given after the tragic loss in 1804 of the 64-gun warship HMS *York* with all of those on board.

The model shows the tower with various apartments, the railway, cranes, boats, and other equipment employed during the construction of the building. Work started in 1807 and was completed in 1811 at a cost of £61,000. This scale model (right) was made under the personal supervision of Robert Stevenson in 1822.

Main picture: View of the gallery showing the *Ellesmere* steam locomotive, Hawthorn and Co., Leith, 1861. **Right:** Bell Rock lighthouse, designed by Robert Stevenson (1772–1850), model, scale 1:33, 1822.

Industry and Empire

The focus of **Industry and Empire** is the Scots at home and abroad, from the late 18th to the early 20th century, a period that saw the rapid growth of the British Empire.

During the 18th century Scotland had become an integral part of the British state, and Scottish creativity in new markets produced a number of crucial developments of the industrial age. By the 1890s the British Empire spanned a quarter of the world's land mass. Scottish products were widely recognised, a renown aided by centuries of travel and emigration by Scots around the globe.

The impact of faster, safer transport and communication brought significant improvement to Scotland and beyond, as areas previously difficult to reach became accessible for both work and leisure.

From a range of manufacturing in Scotland, the industries that rose to prominence were shipbuilding, whisky production and railway engineering. The steam locomotive *Ellesmere* (main picture) dominates this gallery. Built in Leith by Hawthorn and Co. in 1861, its working life lasted until 1957 when it became the oldest steam locomotive still in use in Britain. Railway engineering provided employment for many people, not only during the manufacturing process but also far beyond into the working life of the engines.

Scotland's literary figures, explorers, missionaries and engineers are widely celebrated for their achievements. In **Industry and Empire** we feature some of the most illustrious, including Scotland's national bard Robert Burns, Sir Walter Scott and Robert Louis Stevenson.

Scotland and the World

Scots have a long tradition of travel, trade and exploration extending far beyond Scottish waters. The Scottish Diaspora – those who claim descent from Scotland's emigrants – numbers over 25 million people. During the 18th and 19th centuries, Scots in particular left their homeland in large numbers, travelling further and further afield and leaving a permanent mark on the world.

In this gallery we look at migration and what drove it within Scotland and beyond. There were many push and pull factors, although most often these were often economic. Motivations could range from finding a better way to survive, or to seek one's fortune, or to do Christian missionary work to save souls. The significant impact of the Scots in India, America, Australasia and Africa, both positive and negative, is explored here.

During the 18th and 19th centuries there were many evictions of farm tenants, particularly in the Highlands, as landlords wanted these areas for more profitable sheep farming. This process became known as the Highland Clearances and successive waves of migration from this area depleted communities and left bitter memories.

Those who could afford to do so often emigrated; others headed for working opportunities in the growing cities. The vast influx of rural dwellers and migrants from Ireland and other parts of Europe put great pressure on housing and resources, prompting charitable and public efforts to improve living conditions.

Above: Suit in Ross tartan, originally made and worn for George IV's visit to Scotland, 1822, Scotland, early 19th century. **Opposite:** *Coronach in the backwoods*, painting by George W. Simson, 1859, showing a piper playing a *coronach*, funeral dirge, while his wife weeps, heartbroken at being forced from their home.

Ross tartan suit

This suit was made for Alexander Ross of Invergordon who by 1817 was studying medicine in Edinburgh. Highland dress had been outlawed between 1746 and 1782 following the final Jacobite defeat, so the opportunity to wear a tartan for King George IV's visit to Edinburgh in 1822 represented a huge shift in perceptions of Scottish identities.

A descendant, Donald Munro Ross, emigrated from Inverness to Australia in 1864 and took this Highland outfit with him. It remained there until 1992 when it was brought back to Scotland.

Medal for the Scottish Parliament

At the official opening of the Scottish Parliament on 1 July 1999, medals were presented to the first Members of the Scottish Parliament (MSPs). The medal on the right was given to Iain C. Gray, Labour MSP for Edinburgh Pentlands, who was then Deputy Minister for Health and Community Care.

The medals were commissioned from the Royal Mint by the Opening Ceremony Working Group which was set up to advise the Scottish Office, and collected by the MSPs after the first summer recess. Similar, smaller medals were also presented to every baby born in Scotland on that day.

Ten years later the Scottish Parliament marked the anniversary with a ceremony led by the Queen and most of the 163 children born on that day.

Main picture: View of the gallery showing a model of an oil platform and section of oil pipeline, part of the Elgin/ Franklin field which began production in 2001. **Right:** Medal, commemorating the opening of the Scottish Parliament, 1999.

Scotland: A Changing Nation

This is Scotland's recent story. From the watershed of the Great War of 1914–18 to the present day, this gallery traces Scotland's political and cultural reinvention, highlighting some of the challenges and delights of life in modern Scotland through objects, personal stories, poetry, song, music and film.

Scotland and its people were deeply affected by the two World Wars, which brought dramatic political, economic and social change. Objects and stories from Scotland's industries – some of them lost and fondly remembered, some traditional, and the new and currently thriving – help to illustrate change and continuity.

Stories are told of some of the people who fought early in the 20th century for women's suffrage and for workers' rights; and there are much more recent accounts of those who worked for the reconvening of the Scottish Parliament. Iconic sporting objects and three short films – Innovation, Business and Culture – help to illustrate contemporary issues.

Stories of the changes in daily life of the people in Scotland are also told – in the home, in shopping habits, in health, leisure and culture. A space within the gallery is devoted to 'Leaving Scotland', to the more than two million people who have emigrated during the 20th century; and in 'One Nation, Five Million Voices' we hear the voices of people in Scotland today.

Adventure Planet

In **Adventure Planet**, on Level 5, you can unearth a range of interesting animals in our interactive nature gallery, take part in a 'dino-dig', go under the sea, in the jungle, or dress up to explore the extreme environment in the Arctic. Measure yourself against a stegosaurus, or identify mystery animals from their smells and other clues, and find out what camouflage you need to hide from predators.

Imagine

Imagine, on Level 1, is designed for families with young children. In the gallery you will be able to make music, tell stories and create art inspired by real objects from around the world. You can invent your own shadow puppet tale, or get cosy in our story corner with books, story bags and puppets. You can also try on outfits from different cultures, or find some friends to help you make a Chinese dragon dance.

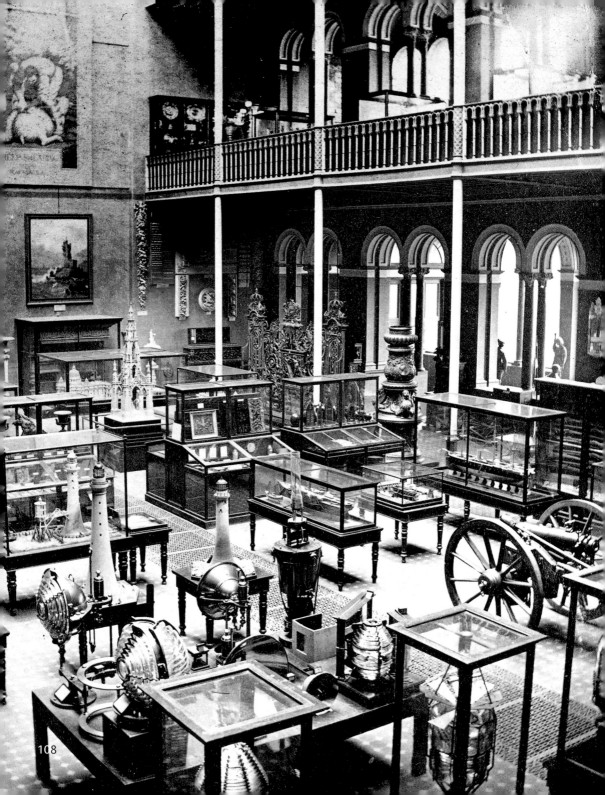

A Short History

The National Museum of Scotland houses a multi-disciplinary and internationally important collection that originates primarily in the 18th and 19th centuries.

The establishment of the Industrial Museum of Scotland in 1854 was followed by the opening of the building on the Chambers Street site in 1866, renamed the Edinburgh Museum of Science and Art. The traditions of international collecting, public education and research were established from the beginning, under the founding Director, George Wilson (1818–59).

The current National Museum of Scotland has a history rooted not only in Wilson's pioneering vision, but also in the University of Edinburgh's earlier Museum of Natural History, the Royal Society of Edinburgh and the former National Museum of Antiquities of Scotland. In 1780 the Society of Antiquaries of Scotland was brought into being by its founder David Steuart Erskine, 11th Earl of Buchan, gaining a Royal Charter in 1783. These collections came into the public sphere in 1858 as the founding collection of the National Museum of Antiquities of Scotland, which were housed from 1891 in galleries alongside the Scottish National Portrait Gallery on Queen Street.

Over the 20th century, contemporary collecting, exchanges and transfers resulted in the growth of the collection. This was perhaps most fully cemented in 1985 by the amalgamation with the National Museum of Antiquities of Scotland to form the National Museum of Scotland. A striking modern wing was commissioned to house the Scottish collections, and this was opened in 1998.

Today the organisation that is National Museums Scotland manages four museums, with the National Museum of Scotland as its flagship, and cares for collections that number over 12 million objects. From 2004 attention returned to the renovation of the Victorian building. Collections held in storage behind the scenes were moved to the National Museums Collection Centre in north Edinburgh. This permitted the opening up of a street-level entrance.

In 2011 the World Cultures and the Natural World galleries were opened. Today, with the Art, Design and Fashion and Science and Technology galleries being reopened in 2016, the Museum can now celebrate the unique diversity of its holdings.

Opposite: The Main Hall of the Edinburgh Museum of Science and Art, c.1868.

Information

National Museum of Scotland

Chambers Street
Edinburgh, EH1 1JF
www.nms.ac.uk/scotland

Open daily: **10.00–17.00**
Admission **free**, donations welcome
For information and bookings, call: **0300 123 6789**

We rely on your donations to care for Scotland's national collections and keep many of our inspiring events and experiences free. Please support us by becoming a Member or making a donation today. Thank you.

Make a donation

To make a donation, please visit:
www.nms.ac.uk/donate or text **NMOS16 £3** to **70070** to donate £3.

Do more with Membership

Membership gives a year of unlimited free entry to our world-class exhibitions, free entry to three museums and a 10% discount on admission to Edinburgh Castle for the National War Museum. Members also get free or reduced entry to a huge range of special events, 20% discount in our cafés and 10% off in our shops.

Join at an information desk today or visit:
www.nms.ac.uk/membership

National Museums Scotland

National Museum of Scotland, Edinburgh
National War Museum, Edinburgh Castle
National Museum of Flight, East Lothian
National Museum of Rural Life, East Kilbride

Visitor information

Learning Centre

The Learning Centre is our hub of inspiring activities for all ages. See the information screens at the Museum or ask staff for details of what's on.

School, college and all group visits

For information, contact:
www.nms.ac.uk/about-us/contact-us/#visits

Eating and drinking

Our **Balcony Café** and **Museum Brasserie** are open daily from 10.00–17.00 for tea, coffee, home-baking, snacks and meals. Call the **Brasserie** on **0131 247 4040** to book a table. The rooftop **Tower Restaurant and Terrace** is open all day, 10am–11pm (last entry), for brunch, lunch, afternoon tea and dinner: reservations can be made on **0131 225 3003**.

Shopping

Visit our shops to buy something to remind you of your visit. We have an extensive selection of imaginative gifts, souvenirs, toys and books. You can also shop online at:

www.nms.ac.uk/shop

Research Library

Explore the collections in depth in our **Research Library** on Level 3.

Access

Wheelchair loan, special tours and handling sessions are available by arrangement.
For more information, visit:

www.nms.ac.uk/access

Events and entertaining

From dinners to private exhibition views, conferences to weddings, we can deliver a great event in our stunning spaces. Call **0131 247 4113** or visit:

www.nms.ac.uk/hospitality

Keep in touch

Sign up for our e-bulletins at:

www.nms.ac.uk/signup

Acknowledgements

While every effort has been made to acknowledge correct copyright of images and objects where applicable, any unintentional omissions or errors should be notified to the Publisher, who will arrange for corrections to appear in subsequent editions.

All images © National Museums Scotland were taken by NMS Photography, unless otherwise credited (see below):

Pages 8–9 Crowds in the Grand Gallery, image Sean Bell, © National Museums Scotland; 12 Window on the World installation, image © Malcolm Cochrane; 18–19 Cast of *Tyrannosaurus rex*, image © Andrew Lee; 20 Lion family, image supplied by Service Graphics, © National Museums Scotland; 22 Elephant, image supplied by Service Graphics, © National Museums Scotland; 22–23 Sika deer, tiger and python, image © Rob McDougall; 26–27 Wildlife Panorama, image Sean Bell, © National Museums Scotland; 31 Earth and Space gallery, image © Andrew Lee; 34–35 Prayer Wheels, image Sean Bell, © National Museums Scotland; 36 Figures and Camp Dogs, © Wally Pwerle, image © National Museums Scotland; 37 World Culture galleries, image © Robert McDougall; 40 Battle Dress, © Vanessa Paukeigope Jennings, Kiowa/Tohono O'odham, 2007, image © National Museums Scotland; 44–45 Stern post, © George Nuku, image © National Museums Scotland; 47 *Devil and Angel*, © Maryam Salour, image © National Museums Scotland; 48–49 *Trance*, © Preston Singletary, image © National Museums Scotland; 49 Preston Singletary, image © Hulleah J. Tsinhnahjinnie; 49 Kondō Takahiro with works from 'Orkney' series, Tokyo, 2008, © Yamazaki Kenichi; 54 Hamilton-Rothchild tazza: Accepted by HM Government in lieu of Inheritance Tax and allocated to National Museums Scotland 2012, image © National Museums Scotland; 58 *Antares* by M. de Lucchi (1983), *Altair* by E. Sottsass (1982); *Alpha Centauri* by M. Zanini (1982) – edited by Memphis srl, Milano, image © National Museums Scotland; 59 Brooch, © Giovanni Corvaja, image © National Museums Scotland; 66–67 and 81 Accelerating cavity from CERN's Large Electron Positron collider (LEP), operational from 1989–2000. Donation by CERN, image © National Museums Scotland; 77 Scale model of Queensferry crossing, © R. G. Model Services Ltd, image © National Museums Scotland; 86 Hilton of Cadboll stone, image Sean Bell, © National Museums Scotland; 87 Engine being maintained in gallery, image Sean Bell, © National Museums Scotland; 89 Model of *Westlothiana lizziae*, by M. I. Coates, image © National Museums Scotland; 93 Mary, Queen of Scots, cast of tomb, Scottish National Portrait Gallery, Edinburgh, image © National Museums Scotland; 104–105 Model of oil platform and pipeline, on loan courtesy of TOTAL E & P Limited, image Sean Bell, © National Museums Scotland; 105 Parliamentary medal, by kind permission of the Royal Mint, © National Museums Scotland; 106 Adventure Planet, image Sean Bell, © National Museums Scotland; 107 Imagine, © Malcolm Cochrane.

With thanks to David Souden, Past Present Ltd.

National Museums Scotland
Scottish Charity, No. SC011130